Pineys

Yael Aravah

Pineys

The People of the
New Jersey Pine Barrens

South Jersey Culture & History Center, 2024

PINEYS: THE PEOPLE OF THE NEW JERSEY PINE BARRENS
By Yael Aravah

Text and photographs copyright © November 2022 and 2024 by Yael Aravah.
Layout copyright © 2024 by the South Jersey Culture & History Center.

All rights reserved. No part of this work may be reproduced or transmitted in any form by any means, electronic or mechanical, including photocopying and recording, or by any information storage or retrieval system without permission in writing from the publisher, except in the case of brief quotations embodied in reviews and certain other non-commercial uses permitted by copyright law.

Printed in U.S.A.

stockton.edu/sjchc/

ISBN: 978-1-947889-24-8

Prologue

In December 2019, I found myself in the Pine Barrens of New Jersey without even knowing that I was in the Pines and without any knowledge of its significance. I had just arrived from Israel when a family member offered me temporary housing in South Jersey. That is how I ended up in Southampton Township, where the pristine forests and picturesque lakes of the New Jersey Pine Barrens surrounded me.

My arrival coincided with the outbreak of the COVID-19 pandemic and the onset of many months of near total isolation. I did not know a soul in the Pines and with the towns on lockdown, I headed for the forests – hiking daily with my two dogs: Alchina, a Mastino Napolitano, and Juna, a Cannan rescue dog from the mountains of Jerusalem. Talking to the trees, conversing with the wildlife, I fell in love with the Pine Barrens.

A seventeenth-century Japanese poet, Matsuo Basho, wrote that "Every day is a journey and the journey itself is home." My daily journeys had become actual treks of discovery into this beautiful wilderness. The Pine Barrens had become my home. At the end of each day, I would return to the comfort of my township accommodations. Living conditions in the "Barrens," however, have long been considered inhospitable, its inhabitants considered the dregs of society. The American Piney story is a fascinating one, though one that the current crop of historians and sociologists of Americana have ignored.

The Pineys are the rustic forest dwellers in the New Jersey Pine Barrens, and in many ways, people treated them like the Hillbillies of Appalachia. Early Pineys included fugitives, poachers, moonshiners, runaway slaves, deserting soldiers, and some remaining natives from the local Lenape bands. Some sustained themselves through collecting and selling sphagnum moss and pinecones. Others hunted, fished, cut lumber, and produced charcoal. Those who could, eked out a living farming the barren land. As the name would suggest, the poor soil of the Pine Barrens is rather unsuitable for agriculture. Some Pineys resorted to bootlegging and rumrunning. Those locally known as the "Pine Robbers" made their living by banditry, particularly during the Revolutionary War.

In the early part of the twentieth century, pseudo-scientists subjected Pineys to mistreatment and discrimination. Elizabeth Kite, from the Vineland School, created many of the stereotypes by conducting questionable genealogical research and developing such derogatory terms as "piney" and "moron."

In 1912, Henry Herbert Goddard published *The Kallikak Family: A Study in the Heredity of Feeble-Mindedness*. Amongst his findings were recommendations of compulsory sterilization and segregation for Pineys as temporary emergency measures. Adolf Hitler and the Third Reich embraced this excursion into Eugenics research as a rationale for the Master Race concept. Though the research of both Goddard and Kite was eventually proven false, the stigma remained, and the then acting New Jersey Governor, James F. Fielder, a Democrat from Jersey City, adopted the recommendations and proposed the sterilization of the Pineys in the early 1900s, although the state never moved forward with the plan.

Goddard did not confine his obsession to define various ethnic groups as feebleminded to just the Pines. Goddard claimed that 80 percent of Jewish, Hungarian, Italian, and Russian immigrants were also feebleminded. His specious findings contributed to successful efforts to pass the Immigration Restriction Act of 1924, which practically eliminated Jewish immigration into the United States.

As a Jew, I have a sentiment for people who suffered from demonization and dehumanization, and as a documentary filmmaker, I decided to tell this story. As part of my research for the film, I have been meeting many locals and asking them questions such as, "Do you consider yourself a Piney?" and "What does being a Piney mean to you?" Their various responses and viewpoints have been gathered in this book, *Pineys,* as part of the greater "Do You Consider Yourself a Piney?" project. These interviews have taught me, among many other things, that the word Piney still persists as an insult and slur. While some are in denial or are ashamed of their heritage, others are making it a statement of pride. Some are even making it their profession, becoming "professional Pineys."

Nowadays, there is a small but growing "Proud to be Piney" movement with a mandate to change the notion of what it is to be a Piney. Today, they tend to wear the label as a badge of honor, much like the term "Redneck" has been embraced in the southern United States. The Pineys I have met, for the most part, have been open, honest, and incredibly interesting. I like them very much and appreciate them for inviting me in to take quite an intimate look into their world. With my book, I hope to provide the reader with an authentic glimpse into their life in The Pines.

The descriptor **Piney** is a historically derogatory term for inhabitants of the New Jersey Pine Barrens. Living conditions in the "Barrens" were considered inhospitable, and many people considered those who lived there the dregs of society: fugitives, poachers, moonshiners, runaway slaves, or deserting soldiers. Their often poor economic standing forced Pineys to make a living in any way possible. They collected and sold sphagnum moss or pinecones, hunted, fished, and lived off the land. During the eighteenth century, some of the Pineys included notorious bandits known as the "Pine Robbers," groups of loosely organized criminal gangs and marauders sympathetic to the British, serving as Loyalists during the American Revolutionary War.

They used the New Jersey Pine Barrens to hide while they wreaked havoc in the area. The Pine Barrens' densely forested terrain created concealment where guerrilla and criminal activities could easily be carried out. Today, Pineys tend to wear the label as a badge of honor, much like the term "redneck" has been embraced in the Appalachian Mountains and the southern United States.

The Pine Barrens is a large and heavily forested area that stretches across the southern coastal plain of New Jersey and is renowned for its unspoiled nature, and its abundant and diverse flora and fauna. Also known as the Pinelands, it covers a huge area of over 1.1 million acres, or 22 percent of New Jersey's landmass, with only 400,000 people living in it.

In 1979, New Jersey formed a partnership with the federal government to preserve, protect, and enhance the natural and cultural resources of this special place. Congress created the Pinelands National Reserve (PNR) through the passage of the National Parks and Recreation Act of 1978. The PNR is the first National Reserve in the United States. In 1988, UNESCO designated the New Jersey Pine Barrens as a single-site Biosphere Region, elevating the area to an international status.

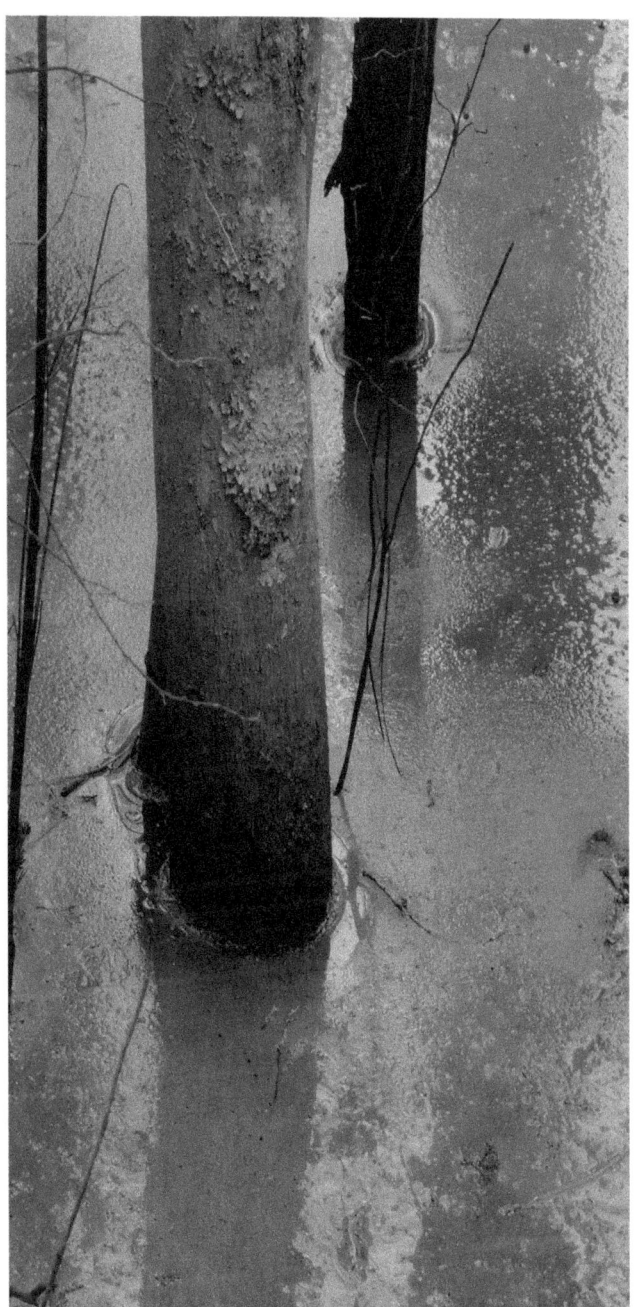

Harry

"A Piney from my head to my Hiney"

"To be a Piney is akin to an expression of profanity, similar to being called a Hillbilly from the Smoky Mountains. Ill-founded rumors once suggested that Pineys procreated with their siblings and sometimes their children. That they also ate people and performed other similar uncivilized acts. The Pineys seem to have gained that reputation. In truth, it likely originated from nothing more than 'old wives tales.'"

Darrell

"I was born and lived here all my life as a Piney. We live off the land, go hunt for deer meat and share it and eat. Mom used to make bread and we share it."

Jen

Primitive Piney

"Of course, I consider myself a Piney. I wouldn't know what else to consider myself.

For me, it's more like a connection to the land, like I grew up here. You know, it's like my religion, my temple, my church, my home. It's a place where I feel at peace."

Cedar water that flows through the Pinelands is evidence of the area's biodiversity. The water's light brown hue is a result of the tannic acids present in the Pines' plant life – especially the Atlantic white cedar – as well as naturally occurring iron in many of the streams.

The Pine Barrens are home to many plants that are officially listed as threatened or endangered due to their rarity in the state, the nation, or the world.

King among the gymnosperms of the Pine Barrens is the Pitch Pine, the single most characteristic plant species of this ecosystem.

The **Jersey Devil** (also known as the Leeds Devil)

The New Jersey Pinelands is home to acres of pine trees and miles of sandy roads, but it also serves as the home of New Jersey's most infamous denizen, the **Jersey Devil**. For more than 250 years this mysterious creature has reputedly prowled the marshes and periodically rampaged through towns and cities.

The creature is often described as a flying biped with hooves, but there are many variations. The common description is that of a bipedal kangaroo-like or wyvern-like creature with a horse or goat-like head, leathery bat-like wings, horns, small arms with clawed hands, legs with cloven hooves, and a forked tail. It reportedly moves very quickly.

Due to numerous recountings over the years of the various claimed instances of sightings, the Jersey Devil legend has many variations. The most widely held belief about its origin is that Mrs. Leeds, a resident of Estellville, Atlantic County, became distraught when she learned that she was expecting for the thirteenth time. In disgust, she cried out, "let it be the devil!" The story continues that the child arrived, and it was a baby devil. The creature immediately gave a screech, unfolded its wings, and flew out the window or up the chimney and into the swamp.

Growing up in the Barrens, one is typically exposed to the Jersey Devil mythos at an early age. Research by Carol Johnson and David Munn revealed that prominent citizens or government officials were among many who had witnessed sightings of the creature in the mass hysteria of 1909. This marked the beginning of the change from local folklore to the devil's presence in regional culture.

AI work of the Jersey Devil, opposite page, by Adam Shuldman.

Paul Evans Pederson Jr.

Born and raised in southern New Jersey, Paul fell in love with the Pine Barrens in 1962, and now makes it his home. On his first camping trip he and his fellow campers believe they encountered the Jersey Devil.

Paul is an artist and has become a legend of the Pine Barrens himself. He writes and recounts Pine Barrens legends through books and musical performances. He is an accomplished songwriter, performer, screenwriter, and photographer.

A collector of antique glass bottles, he produces jewelry from the glass under the product line of "Pine Barrens Diamonds." Paul is a great storyteller and sings while playing the drums and/or guitar. He is also a professional firefighter.

"I am a Piney."

"A Piney girl, and I say that with pride. I know it is associated with having a closed mind, but that is simply not true.

I consider myself as a Piney girl because I love the outdoors and nature is very much my thing. As well as this, my family heritage is intertwined in this special location and lifestyle and it's important to me.

My own grandfather was connected to the Leeds family, and I believe in that story that the Jersey Devil is their son."

The New Jersey Pine Barrens has been the site of many legends, tales, and mythical creatures. The Jersey Devil, Captain Kidd, the Black Dog, the Golden-Haired Girl, the Black Doctor, and the White Stag are some of them.

Dave

When I asked Dave if he considers himself a Piney, he said:

"Oh Yeah," and then added: "I think that's like asking if someone is a biker.

It's something that lives inside in your heart, it's a place you like to be and it's a place you'd like to be back to. And these people have the same love.

I am originally from Riverton, and I was the boy scout who told all the Jersey devil's stories around the campfire, most of us then did not even know what a Piney was but we knew it's something that was frightening. You didn't know what it was but I decided I had to find it, now it lives in here. I don't know how else to describe it. it's a feeling really. You get out there and you feel home."

Charles

"We never got hungry because we know how to survive off the woods. We made our living off the woods, we cut bark, we collected pinecones – everything was worth money. My mom and dad had a tough life. We lived deep in the woods. No neighbors or nothing."

Millie

"A true Piney can wipe his butt with a cranberry leaf.

The family here raised 12 kids. The house did not have any plumbing at all. The family took turns bathing in the same bath. They didn't have a toilet in the house, but instead made-do with a chamber pot. The kids would empty this outside."

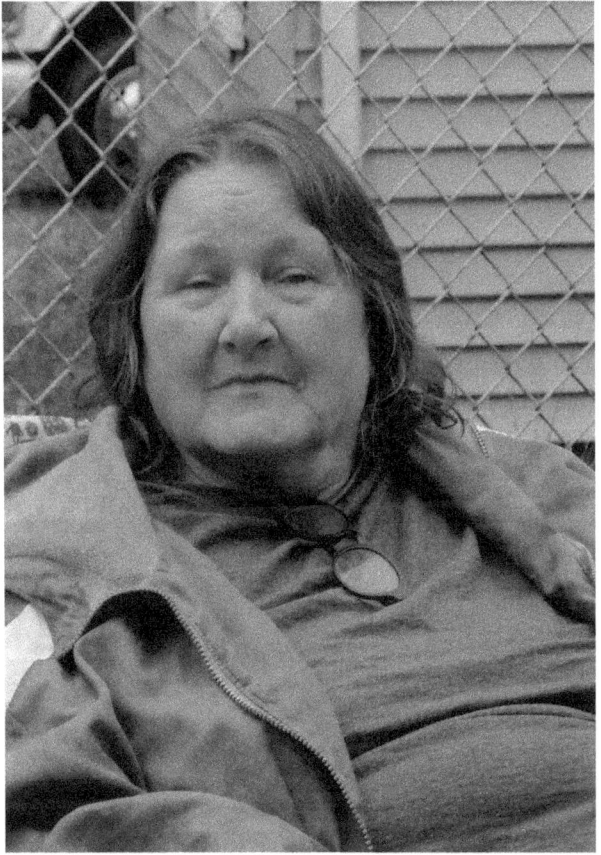

Indian tribes considered piebald deer to be embodiments of spirits passing to or from the spirit world. Seeing a piebald deer meant that *change was coming*.

James

"Maybe in the modern terminology yes, I am a Piney, but not so much in the traditional sense. In the traditional Piney, whose family has been in the pine for generations, another key feature would be that they worked the seasons; they don't just have the same job all year round. When it's blueberry season, they are picking blueberries. When it is pine season, they gather pinecones, or collecting sphagnum moss in its time.

The piney was originally or became sort of a derogatory term, but it seems like the people who love the Pines are taking this name back. Now they say it in pride, so in that regard a Piney today is someone who loves the pines and is crazy about it, so I fit that."

Bob

"Pine Barrens was not in the past an identity, but an actual place called the Pine Barrens. I would say that I am a person of native descent from The Pines.

The Pines and its culture are more protected these days. And, whereas the outside world changed, the Piney culture stayed the same. I am a Piney, and this is my protection for my own identity.

My own father would take me to play the fiddle, and these were in places within the Pines. He would not say, 'this is Piney culture…' He would just call it 'Old timer culture.' There was a period when they wanted to segregate the Pineys.

They didn't end up doing this, but they did take folks out of the community. Mostly it was those with 'black blood' and 'native Indian blood.' They were then placed in four towns along the Delaware river. I won't mention which particular towns these are, because these communities are still there. Secretly! But if you were to ask them if they are Pineys, they would say no. They would say that they are of native descent from the Pines and that is how I originally saw myself. I do think that we have to become a Piney to survive and have protection so that we don't become assimilated into regular society."

Arney

"NO! I am not a Piney. A Piney is someone who lives down here in the fields. But really, they don't appreciate the word Piney as it is thought of as derogatory and inflammatory and things like that. They have names, like us. I don't call people from the city 'city slickers'; it's a derogatory name. I call them by their real names."

Rob

"Yes, I am a Piney and I am proud of it. Both sides of my family going back to the 1700s was full Pineys, and I was born here next to the sawmill."

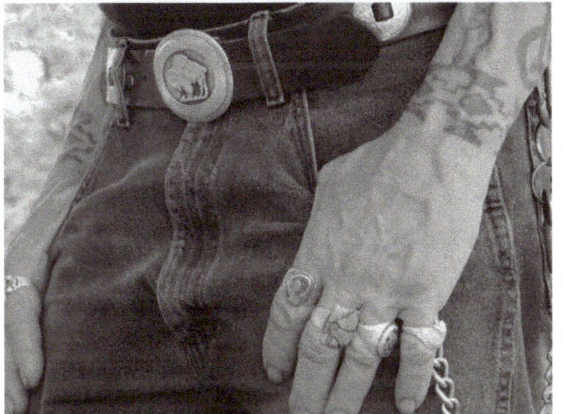

Indian Tom

Do you consider yourself a Piney?

"I am an American."

Man has inhabited the Pinelands for at least 2,000 years, although archaeologists have found evidence of human occupation as far back as the end of the ice age. While European settlement of the Pinelands occurred in the late seventeenth century, members of the Lenape tribe, meaning "original people," who the Europeans renamed the Delaware Indians, had been living in southern New Jersey, including the Pine Barrens, for several centuries.

The Lenape fished in the ocean and bays and in the rivers of the Pinelands; farmed and raised animals; and hunted and foraged for food and other necessities in the woodlands. Their lifestyle left the natural features of the Pinelands – wooded areas, swamps, meadows, and bays – largely unchanged. They shared their traditional ways of using and adapting to the environment of the Pinelands with the early European settlers, who learned how to cultivate maize, and what items to forage for food and other necessities. Many of the Lenape succumbed to smallpox and other diseases, against which they had no immunity, as a result of their contact with the Europeans who brought these diseases. Other members of the tribe moved out of the area or resettled on one of the earliest Indian reservations, the Brotherton Reservation, later renamed Indian Mills.

Lenape bands practiced companion planting, in which their women cultivated many varieties of plants of the "Three Sisters" crops, which were maize, beans, and squash. Women also were often skilled at basket-weaving. Men practiced hunting and the harvesting of seafood. By the time the Europeans first arrived, the Lenape were cultivating fields of vegetation through the slash and burn technique.

Indian Ann walked many miles to sell her lovely baskets. She was the last native women to produce such crafts.

Mary

"The Lenape Indian tribe used to live on this land, one of their crafts was weaving baskets. My basket-weaving just came to me naturally. It's part of my Lenape ancestry passed to me as a Piney. I am connected to the Pine Barrens through my father and his ancestors, the Bozarths. They were Pineys and lived off the land. Most of the food came from hunting deer, squirrels, and muskrat."

Joe

"I consider myself somewhat of a Piney. I was not born and raised here, but I love the Pinelands and I come here as often as I can and to me that is a Piney. Some people think a Piney is someone just born here, lived here, and lives off the land here, and does everything as a Piney.

But I do consider myself somewhat of a Piney."

Wayne

"Me, I am not a Piney. I wasn't born and raised here. Piney is someone who's born and raised here. I am from North Jersey where the horrible rat race is. Back then it was all farmlands, but no longer. Now it's all condos and buildings. My wife was born and raised here; she is a Piney, I guess. But if you live here more than 20 years you become an honorary Piney. So, I guess I must now be one because I have lived here since 1979, so I think I am considered a Piney. Some call 'Piney' to a guy that has no teeth. I guess they stay here in the area; they never leave. They lived off the land. It's about people that just basically love their surroundings and they like living in the woods and live from the land."

Elaine

"My father grew up there and all of his ancestors are buried there. My great, great grandfather, Nicholas Sooy, owned Green Bank and built the Green Bank Methodist Church, so I guess I count as a Piney. My great grandfather, Charles Green, was a lay minister at what is now called Pinelands Methodist Church (at Pleasant Mills and Batsto)."

There are some iconic places that are still around and every Piney knows.

Albert Hall – The sound of the Pinelands

Brothers Joe and George Albert began to hold Saturday night gatherings at the "Homeplace," a deer lodge cabin on 51 acres that the brothers bought during the depression for hunting purposes. In the 1950s, musicians would come and do jam sessions until Sunday morning. The place became widely known and soon hundreds of people were coming to the "Homeplace." They moved to a bigger location in 1974, a Waretown auction building. The place burned down in 1992, so Saturday night shows continued in the parking lot. A new 600-square-foot hall opened in 1996, and it still operates here today. Every Saturday night there are live performances: old music, new music, local music and what no one could define for me yet, Piney music. Devoted volunteers run the place.

Whitesbog Historic Village is a cranberry farming village founded in 1857. Located in Brendan T. Byrne State Forest, it was the largest New Jersey cranberry farm in the early 1900s. Its founder, J. J. White, was a nationally recognized leader in the cranberry industry. Whitesbog, an important part of New Jersey history and blueberry & cranberry culture in the United States, is listed in both the National and State Registers of Historic Sites. It includes the village and the surrounding 3,000 acres of cranberry bogs, blueberry fields, reservoirs, sugar sand roads and Pine Barrens forests.

Whitesbog　　　　　　　　　　　Whitesbog　　　　　　　　　　　Whitesbog

Lucille's　　　　　　　　　　Hot Diggidy Dog　　　　　　　　Buzby's General Store

Albert Hall　　　　　　　　　　Albert Hall　　　　　　　　　　Albert Hall

Lucille's

Lucille Bates was a legendary figure of the Pines. Lucille's Country Cooking is an old-fashioned diner that first opened in 1975 in Warren Grove. Although Lucille died in 2016, visitors still flock to the restaurant for the homemade food she made famous.

Chatsworth

This village is located within Woodland Township, Burlington County. The New Jersey Central Railroad's THE BLUE COMET passenger train wrecked near here in August 1939. Chatsworth carries the moniker of "Capital of the Pine Barrens."

Buzby's General Store, which Neil Wade opened in 1865, and later Willis J. Buzby purchased in 1895, served as a community gathering spot. It closed permanently in 1992 and sold at tax sale in 1998 to Marilyn Schmidt, who thoroughly renovated the venerable old store and reopened it in 2004. Marilyn operated the store until 2017, when advancing age and its infirmities forced her to close. Marilyn passed in February 2019 and the store sold in 2021 to Jason Grater and Edward Strojan Sr., who reopened it in 2022. Today, Buzby's primarily functions as a restaurant. The store is listed in the National and State Register of Historic Places and has always played an important role in the life of the Pines.

One of its owners, Willis Jefferson Buzby would become known as the King of the Pineys. This title would later carry over to his son, Jack. The store was a cornerstone of life in the Pine Barrens; people depended on it for food, clothes, and many other necessities. Willis Buzby's work included banking responsibilities, such as paying local teachers; tax collecting; and medicinal dispensing to Chatsworth residents. He served as host of other social and shopping needs of the community.

Nixon's General Store

Nixon's is another traditional store that seems to have been here forever. Its presence in Tabernacle has lasted for over 100 years, offering residents general goods, snacks, delicious deli food, and more. The store has been passed down from family to family over the years.

Batsto

An old iron furnace and glass town that dates to before the Revolutionary War days. This village is an historic site in the south-central Pinelands of New Jersey. It is known throughout the country, both for its beauty and its historical significance. Batsto has roots dating back to 1766, so it comprises nearly two and a half centuries of American history.

Hot Diggidy Dog

This well-known hotdog stand was established in 1989 in the heart of downtown Chatsworth. It is a happy roadside stand that you can't miss if you pass through Chatsworth on your way to the shore or wandering in the Pines.

Pic-A-Lili Inn

Open since the 1920s, a local story is that one of the owners had a goat that used to drink beer at the bar.

Terry

A Passionate artist, devoted Pine Barrens advocate, volunteer, life-long student of botanical, natural and local history, friend.

"I'd like to feel like I've made a contribution, I've connected people, or I've made someone else appreciate the area that way I have.

Does it make me a Piney? It depends on how people are defining Pineys."

When I asked her how she defines Piney, she replied:

"Whether Piney is accepted as a terminology is not for me to decide, it's an affectionate term to me, it's a respectable term to me."

"I guess I am a transplant Piney," she said, while explaining to me about the importance of native plants because they are adapted to the conditions and the Pines' conditions are very different from other places.

"I've been here since I was one year old, that's over half a century." She reminisces about her mother's love and respect for the Pines and the exploring they did together.

"When I moved to Lower Bank, I met so many people that have so much ancestral history to early New Jersey and I love them all dearly. I love everything I've been taught. I adore it, I love to find the connection between people."

Paul

"There are many people out there who are would-be Pineys, but most fail to fit the traditional tenets of being one. As a professional historian, I have long studied the Pine Barrens and its residents, but I would never refer to myself as a Piney. I love my creature comforts and my library too much to live off the land!"

Paul is the Assistant Director of the South Jersey Culture & History Center at Stockton University.

Mark

Is a plant explorer, and he regularly wanders around looking at different plant habitats.

"I am looking for rare and endangered species," he explains, "I have been raised in the Pines, but that doesn't necessarily make you a Piney. Some people think you need to live off the Pines in order to be a true Piney."

The Sopranos Style

Not only gangsters, but killers of all breeds from New York and Philadelphia disposed of their bodies in the Barrens, apparently lured by the miles of uninhabited woodland and sandy trails. Perhaps the most famous case occurred in 1967, when J. Edgar Hoover, the late F.B.I director, announced what he called a "Cosa Nostra burial farm" had been found in rural Jackson Township, Ocean County.

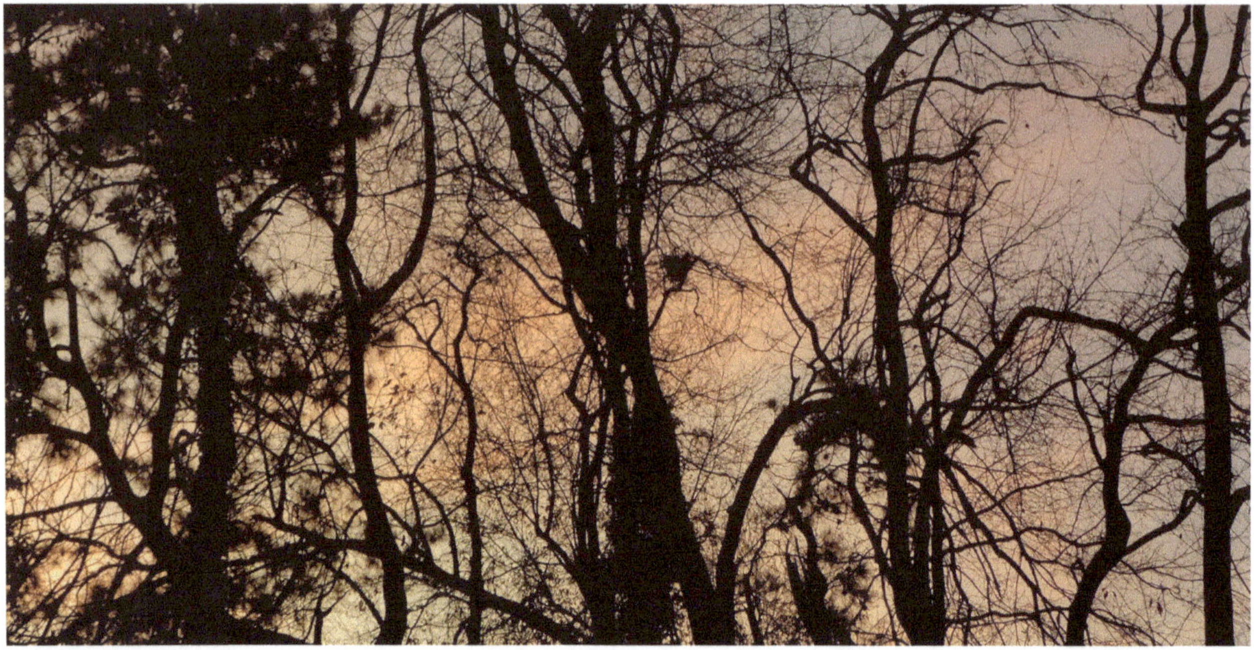

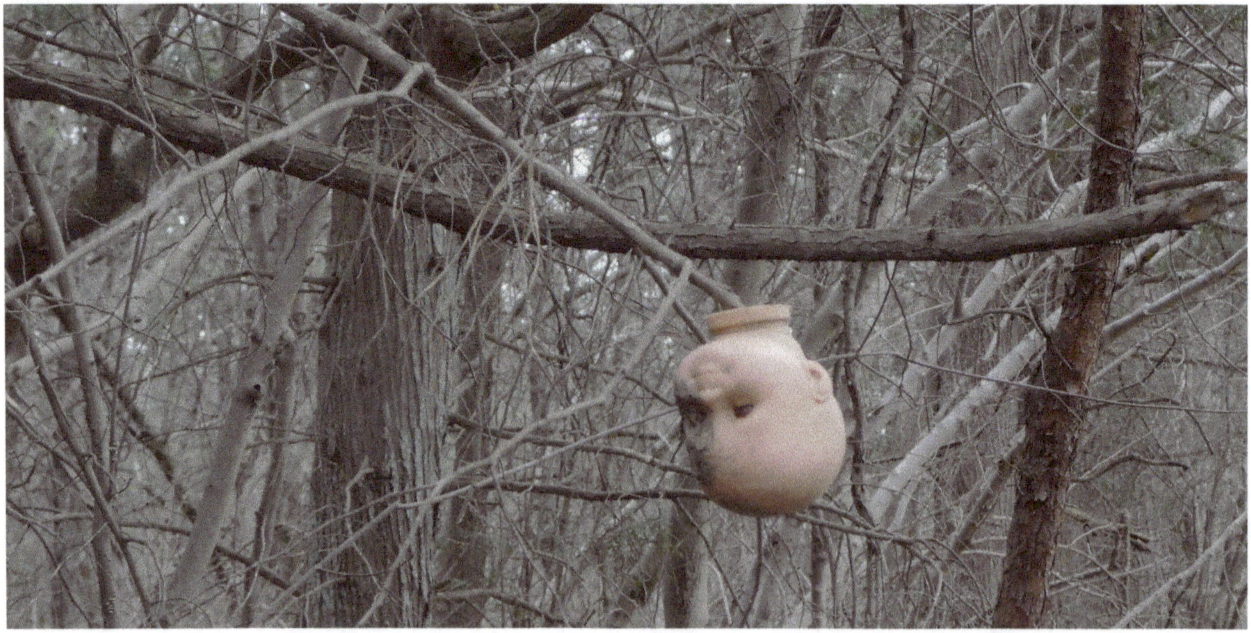

A local joke you can hear in the Barrens: Two mafia hitmen are hiking deep into the forest in the middle of the night. One of them says: "I gotta admit, I'm scared out here." The other replies: "You're scared! . . . I gotta walk back alone!"

The artist **Victoria Kushnir** wearing a "Lawn" dress that she created, inspired by the days of smuggling in the Pine Barrens during the Civil War.

A bone or metal hoop went under the skirt adding to its volume and ability to hide or smuggle contraband through the countryside. The hoop ruse failed after a time when women began to be caught. Stories tell of towns banning the skirts altogether.

In the late nineteenth century, there was steady coverage in *The New York Times* about the act of dress smuggling. This act was often referred to as "fashionable smuggling."

From 1920 until 1933, the United States endured a nationwide constitutional law prohibiting the production, importation, transportation, and sale of alcoholic beverages.

One of the more famous bootlegging gangsters was Al Capone. According to local lore, he relocated to the Pines in 1927. There is little evidence for his life here, but endless stories about him, some involving a basement of alcohol, tunnels for smuggling, and more.

When Prohibition was repealed in 1933, many bootleggers and suppliers with wet sympathies simply moved into the legitimate liquor business.

Routes of the Underground Railroad (UGRR) passed through the New Jersey Pine Barrens serving as a gateway for those escaping enslavement from the South. Some runaway enslaved people crossed the Delaware River to reach Underground Railroad (UGRR) stations in Pennsylvania (Philadelphia), New York (New York City) and Canada (Toronto). Many runaways stayed in New Jersey's numerous all-black communities that served as UGRR sanctuaries, such as Burlington County's Timbuctoo. Burlington County, New Jersey, was of particular significance to the UGRR and the abolitionist movement because it served as a hub for UGRR activities. It was the birthplace of John Woolman, a Quaker abolitionist whose writings helped to turn Quakers against slavery in the late 1700s. It was also the birthplace of black abolitionist, William Still (Father of the Underground Railroad). The State of New Jersey is of great significance to the UGRR movement because of its large number of all-black communities that served as UGRR sanctuaries for escaped slaves.

Frank

"No, I am not a Piney! I grew up in the area, but I came from an Air Force family. I ended up at McGuire Air Force Base when I was 14, and then I stayed here, to be a Piney, I guess. It is to be with no manners, and that's what it seems to me. I call people who don't do things by the book, 'Pineys.'"

Colleen

"Oh yes, I am a Piney! An honorary one; I wasn't born here. My parents moved here in 1955 because it was close to Fort Dix.

I love the Pines! It's special here and I am very worried now because I am afraid it's going to turn now into condos and houses. Army wives sometimes got abandoned here and stayed to raise their children. I love the Pines. If you don't know what a Piney is, you are not a Piney. I am a transplanted Piney. And I love it here.

I remember the real Pineys. When I was a kid, the people used it like it's derogatory. They worked the cranberries, they worked the blueberries. They collected laurels, they collected pinecones for the florist, and they made their way, collecting the dried weeds to sell to the florist. There's nothing derogatory about being a Piney. They're hard-working people, and I could never understand it, and I remember different people that came from Chatsworth and people whispered: 'He is a Piney.' There is nothing wrong with being a Piney. I wasn't born here, but I guess I am a Piney and I am proud to be a Piney. In town, we have churches and bars, and on Fridays people will come to get away from the Pines. They were the real Pineys and I am sure some of them are still around, at least I hope so.

I am thinking the Jersey Devil may be out there in the Pines because the Pine Barrens are so vast and I hope it stays that way. I also think Bigfoot is out there because I heard people that have experienced strange things over the years. I think we don't know the half of what's out there in the Pines."

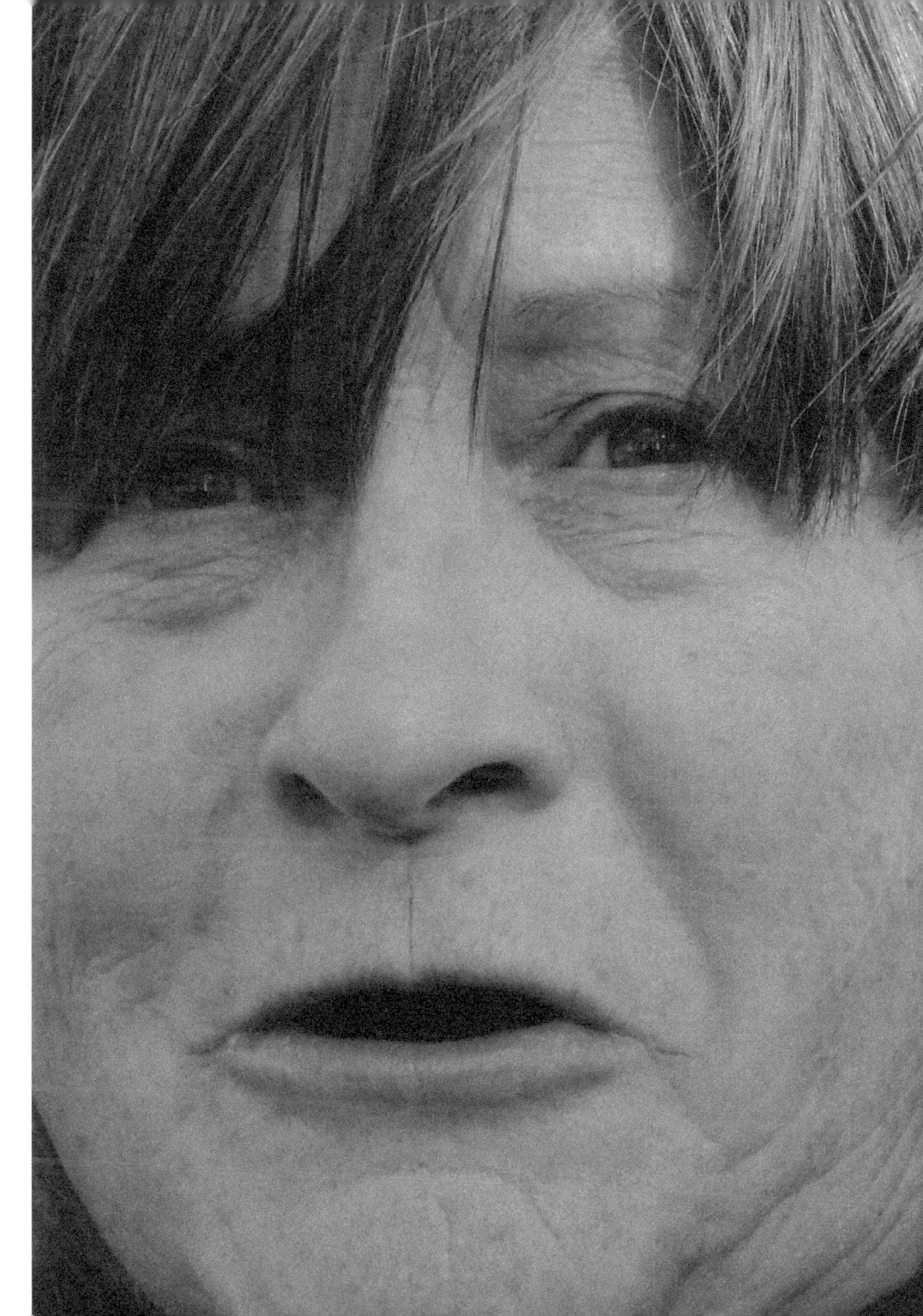

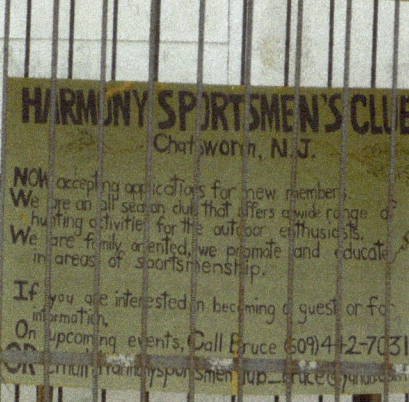

Bill

The Last Piney

Bill Wasiowich is known in the Pine Barrens as "the last Piney." He is a local celebrity – almost a legend. When outsiders, journalists, historians, and filmmakers come to learn about the Pines, they refer to him.

"I'm used to the strangers coming here," he told me when we met in his home. He lives in the front lodge by the entrance to the Crooked Barrel Gun Club in the Pinelands. They have let him live there for decades for the symbolic amount of a thousand dollars a year.

Bill, 83 years old, used to do it all – all the endeavors in which a typical Piney would engage – from hunting, to collecting pinecones, to harvesting cranberries and blueberries, to making wreaths. Nowadays, he still makes wreaths from pinecones he collects and paints. He is still cutting felled trees to sell for firewood, but no longer forages regularly for moisture-rich sphagnum moss that carpets many swamp bogs of the Pines.

The "Last Piney" designation began when he was 28 years old, and John McPhee described him as one of the last Pineys.

John McPhee, American writer

John McPhee wrote a series of articles about the history, people, and biology of the New Jersey Pine Barrens for *The New Yorker* magazine in 1967. In 1968, it was published as a book titled *The Pine Barrens*. His book was important in increasing the awareness of this unique place and its people when the area was under imminent threat for a new regional jetport project.

When I asked Bill if he was really the last Piney, he smiled and said, "I don't know about that. There are more people who live in the woods, but it is hard to find them."

He is growing his own vegetables on a van's roof next to his lodgings. When I asked him for his definition of a Piney, he told me that, "Now they call everybody a Piney. But I can tell you what a legitimate Piney is. A legitimate, South Jersey Piney can trace their family back to the 1700s – some of them, as far back as even late 1600s. A few live in proper houses, some in small makeshift ones, and a handful even live in caves."

"Living in the woods," says Bill, "is a lifestyle."

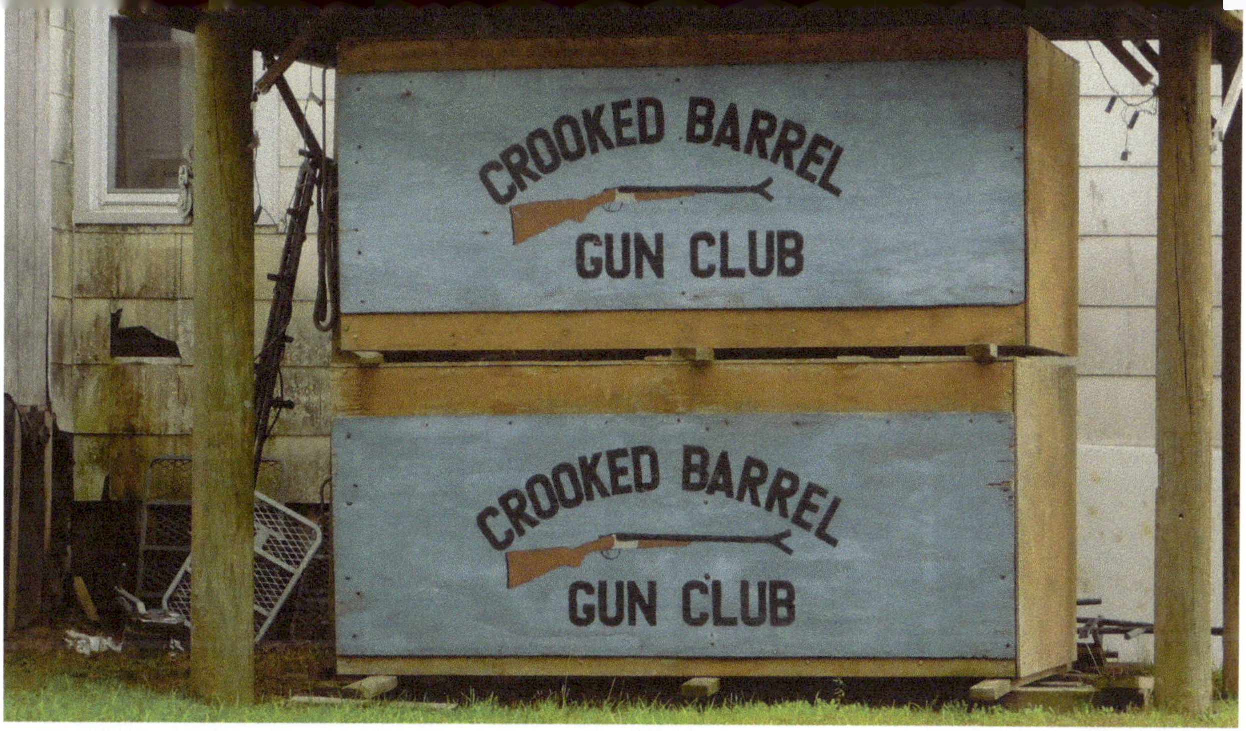
CROOKED BARREL
GUN CLUB
CROOKED BARREL
GUN CLUB

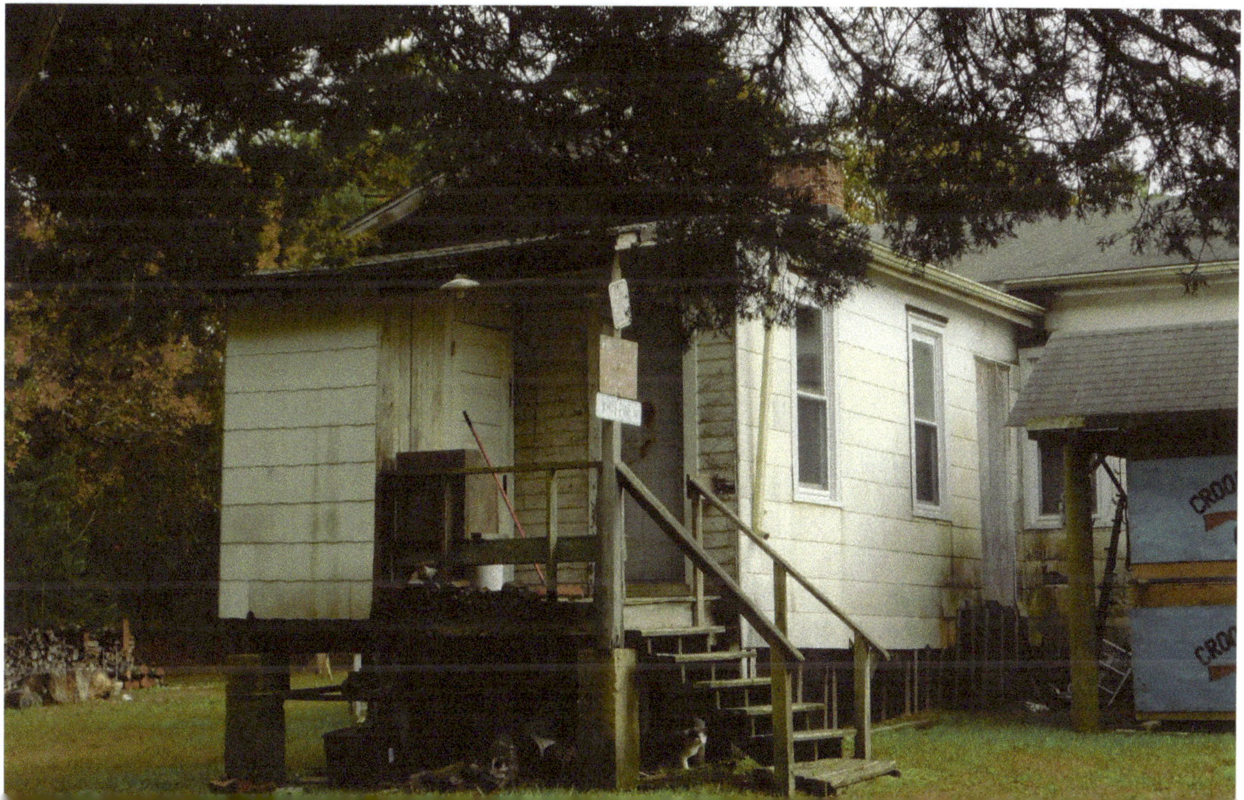

The Pine Barrens is said to be one of the most haunted places in America. The many ruins of ghost towns do tell the stories of the past, and about the thriving towns and villages that once existed here. The ruins are a testament to the places and traditions, some of which continue. Legends, lore, and landmarks abound in the Pinelands. Here are three examples of them:

Harrisville is one of these forgotten towns. It once provided homes to 400 people in the village that contained a paper mill, gristmill, sawmill, homes, and a school that also served as a church on Sundays.

Brooksbrae Brick Factory

Built in 1907 in Manchester Township, Ocean County, the brick factory had the capacity to produce thousands of bricks a day, but likely produced none or perhaps one trial run.

Today it's hidden in the woods and all its remains are covered with a massive amount of graffiti. It has become a place to showcase graffiti art.

There are stories of murder, death, and other spooky tales about this place. Some of them are real and some simply old myths.

Going Nowhere

The Pine Barrens are now home to about a dozen abandoned railroad lines that are going nowhere.

The rails are evidence of the history of the barrens, as they once passed through what we call today ghost towns. Towns that used to provide a decent life during the 18th to 20th centuries and have since faded.

Some of the ghost towns are visible today only as ruins, some known just by their legend, and some can only be spotted by trained eyes.

An old rail line, originally built by the Raritan & Delaware Bay Railroad Company in 1862, abandoned, but still passes through the area and part of the graffiti scene at Brooksbrae.

The way to Atsion

THE BLUE COMET was a Central Railroad of New Jersey passenger train operated from 1929 to 1941 between the New York metropolitan area (Jersey City) and Atlantic City. It passed through the village of Atsion.

When you come to Atsion, it is a ghost town today, but was once a lively village of ironmakers (and other businesses). You will see the impressive mansion, ruins of the Wharton-era concrete stable, the general store, and also a small white church. You would be surprised to learn that the little church still holds services on Sundays. There is a tiny cemetery containing about 200 graves, with some interments dating to the 1830s. A number of markers are devoid of any details as time and the elements have erased them. You will also see a green hunting lodge. That is what is left of Atsion village. If you go on down the trail towards the Batsto River, you then see the old abandoned one-room school building looking back at you from behind the trees. If you continue farther, you will cross the old rail line that formerly carried THE BLUE COMET train. The Quaker Bridge that crosses the Batsto River is still there, too. People come and go for the recreational opportunities the Wharton State Forest has to offer, passing the Atsion Ghost Town, never imagining that this green hunting lodge is the home of "Uncle Stephen" and "Piney Paul." Piney Paul likes to be called a Piney, whereas Uncle Stephen, called by anybody who knows him a "Piney," claims that he is not a Piney at all, because he has been educated. And this shows one of the many ways one can perceive their own identity versus the way others can perceive him.

The philosopher Charles Taylor stated that "We define our identity always in dialogue with, sometimes in struggle against, the things our significant others want to see in us. Even after we outgrow some of these others – our parents, for instance – and they disappear from our lives, the conversation with them continues within us as long as we live."

Quaker's Bridge

The Quaker bridge that spans the Batsto River was built in the late 1770s by members of the Religious Society of Friends. It holds stories of many people and their needs, over many lifetimes during different periods. Some of those tales were written by Jerseyman, the pseudonym of a known local historian, in the Pine Barrens.

Piney Paul told me that I will not find the term "Marshies" in the encyclopaedia, Wikipedia, or the library; it is more an oral form of speech to describe a tradition. It is a person from Gloucester, Salem, or Cumberland county who worked in the marshes, gathering salt hay, hunting muskrats, trapping snapping turtles, etc. The people of the green hunting lodge, the Gloucester County Hunting Club, came up seasonally to hunt deer here. This lodge dates back to the 1760s, before the Revolutionary War. It originally served as an ironworker's residence and was a double house. Two families lived in it.

Gloucester County Hunt Club

The **Atsion Mansion** dates to 1826, when Samuel Richards built it as a summer home. Richards, a prominent ironmaster from Philadelphia, was the owner of the Atsion furnace situated along the Atsion River. The mansion is beautiful, built in the Greek Revival style, which some considered to be iconic of democracy. After Richards died in 1842, the property descended down through his heirs, and finally sold to another Philadelphia merchant, Maurice Raleigh. The Raleigh family was the last to occupy the mansion as a residence. When Joseph Wharton purchased the property in 1892, he used the mansion for packing and storing his cranberry production. The state acquired the property in 1955 as part of the larger Wharton estate purchase.

Grace Bible Baptist Church

Just in front of the lodge stands the still active small white church in the deserted village of Atsion. Every Sunday, about 30 people gather from nearby communities to attend services here.

Uncle Stephen is not taking part in it. "I am not a Baptist," he said. "It used to be an Episcopal church when I was going to services there," he added, "My mom, when she was young girl, did go to this church. And I went to all the services there, too, and I was baptized there."

Piney Paul

People call him "Piney Paul," and he explained to me that it's because he knows a lot about the Pines and always talks about them. "I am a Piney. I lived in the Pines all my life and that's all I know."

"Pineys were doing seasonal jobs, picking blueberries, cranberries, picking pinecones, making grave blankets, making wreaths, collecting cans and metal for money. They hunted and fished, and some had farms."

Steven

"I am considered to be from low-class origins, but I am more educated than that. I come from people that are natives and runaway slaves that once inhabited parts of the Pine Barrens. We have different opinions about who is a Piney and what is a Piney and what makes someone a Piney. And that's okay at the end of the day. There is nothing wrong with that. It is a matter of how you view yourself, and also how other people treat you. Identity is a complicated thing."

"For an example, Uncle Stephen might say that he is not a Piney, even though other people consider him a Piney. It is difficult to really nail down who is a Piney. There is not any academic research which says 'this is a Piney, this is not a Piney.'"

In the closet in the lodge, I saw a bear. Nowadays, the controversial bear hunting is returning to New Jersey.

The name "Atsion" comes from the Lenni Lenape Unami language, a form of Algonquin. It was the name for the strong, cedar-colored stream along which the band called Atsayunk, or Atsiunc, habitated. In late 1765, under Charles Read, Atsion became the site of an iron forge, converting pigs produced from bog iron into malleable iron in pre-Revolutionary times. Later, the furnace and forge manufactured war materiel for the American forces. After the war, the area produced iron stoves and other cast-iron products. The village soon contained a gristmill, sawmills, and, during the mid-nineteenth century, a paper mill was added, subsequently converted into a cotton mill. Still later, Joseph Wharton experimented with growing cotton and peanuts here. An early 1890s icehouse rounded out the facilities at Atsion.

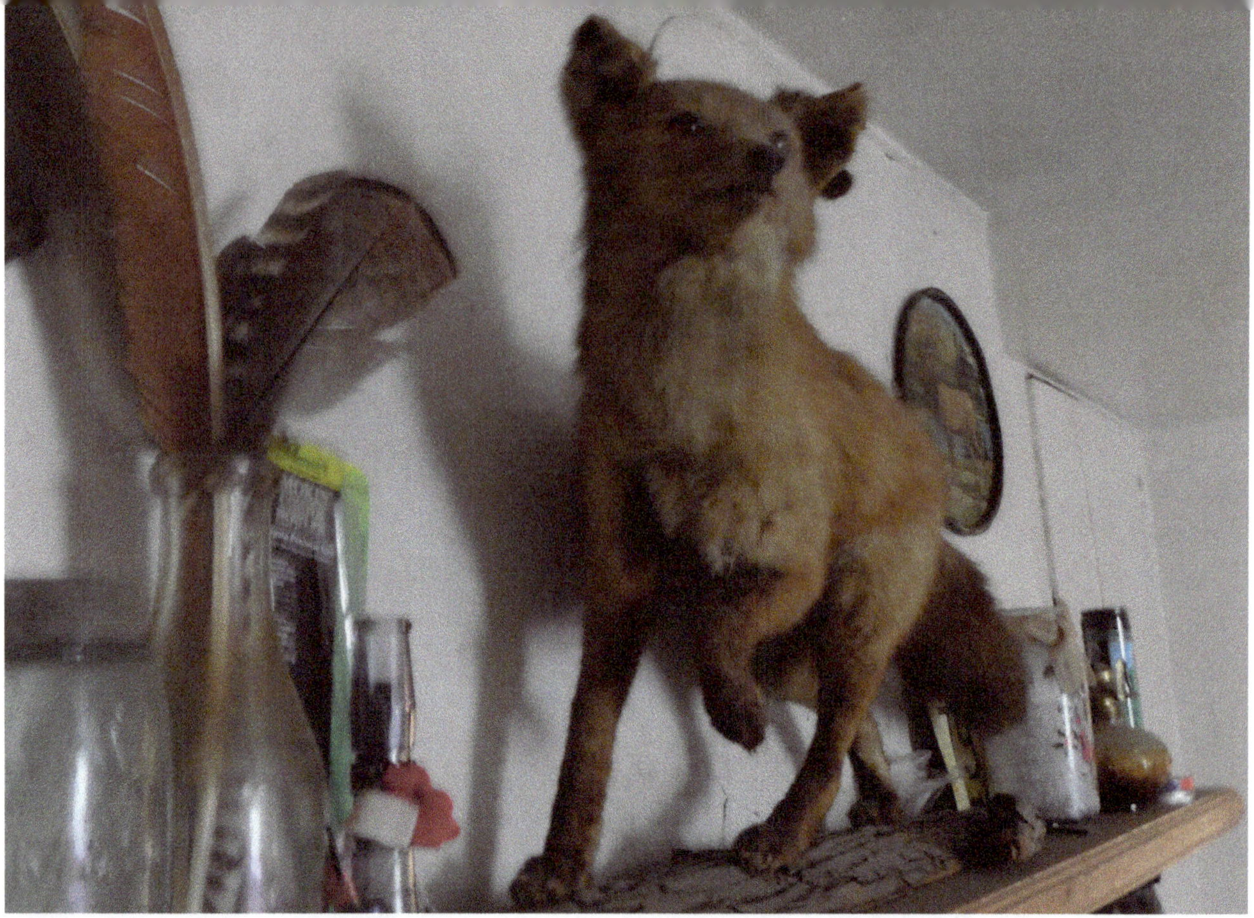

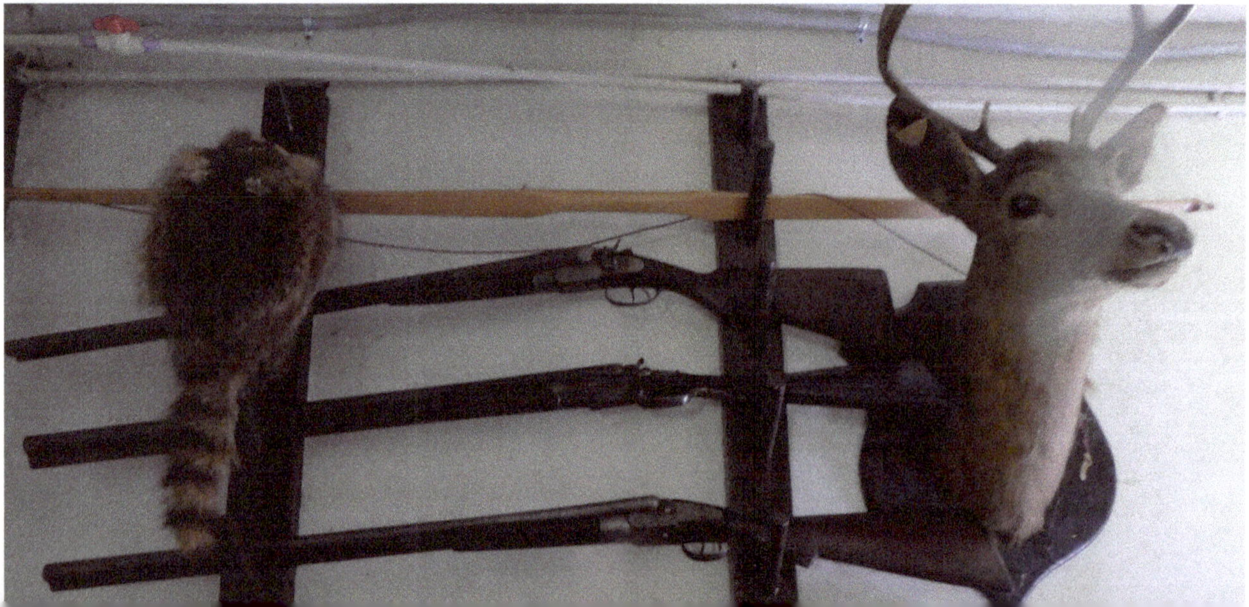

Uncle Stephen

"I tell them I am not a Piney. I am college educated and members of my family went to school.

We have been here since the American Revolution, worked as farmers, and so earned a property in the farmers' district. We are not Pineys.

To me a Piney usually has very little education, if, at all. Some practiced inter-family marriage, if they even bother to marry at all."

When Uncle Stephen was three years old, he moved to Atsion Village to live with his grandparents. Stephen's grandfather was one of the caretakers for the Wharton Estate. He milked the cows and plowed the road with a wagon and wooden Vee-plow. After college, Stephen moved away for a while, but moved back in 1980. Then in 2016 he bought the hunting club and moved into it a short time later.

There are many contributing elements to one's identity.

Some are given at birth: a name, religion, language.

Some are related to the place and time of one's life; many men gain their identity from their profession, social class, and/or the way they dress and talk.

Sometimes, one is defined by the way others perceive him, or by the way he sees his own reflection, and sometimes he views himself through inner self-awareness.

There is an introspection-extrospection mechanism that continually creates and shapes our identity.

Sometimes ethnic groups are subject to demonization and dehumanization in a way that tears and erases their identity as individuals and as a group; they become the scapegoat of society. This practice, steeped in ignorance, forms the foundation of any racism and discrimination, and only knowledge can deconstruct it and lead to healing.

Getting to know who the real people are, and hearing their individual stories, is a pathway to such knowledge, and a part of collective healing.

Acknowledgments

To my beloved and amazing daughter, Gal Shuldman, without whom I wouldn't be able to survive this three-year journey; to her beloved partner, Corey Anderson, who is always supportive behind the scenes. To my beloved talented son, Adam Shuldman, and my beloved special daughter, Ron Nussbaum, who encouraged me to take photos of the barrens and create this book.

To my dear old friend, Orna Hareuveni, who was there for me in many ways when it was tough. And it was tough. To my dear old friend, Michael Zentner, who always supports my dreams, and believed in this project, when it was only a vague idea! To my dear friend Steven Carty who helped tremendously with the research for this book.

To historian Paul W. Schopp, who knows everything about the Pine Barrens, for sharing his knowledge humbly. And for his consulting and editing.

To Judith Anenberg, my angel, and to a heart of gold, Mosh Cohen Moran, for all the help. To my dear friend, Jen, for being Jen. I love your (Primitive) Piney ways! To Adam, again, for the unique edition of the Jersey Devil you created for this book. To my dear friend, Aleja Estronza, who patiently walked me through the way of technology and believed I would be good at this after this project. (I am not.) To my dear old friend Justin Ford (the wind). To Shay Shohat for introducing me to the area. To Alfred Shmuel for his help.

Special thanks to Tom Kinsella, Professor of Literature and Director of the South Jersey Culture & History Center at Stockton University, for embracing this project. I am thankful for the many editing interns who had a hand in producing this book: Olivia Murawski, Frank Wendling, who completed initial layout; and Alice Watt, who worked on layout and on the cover; and the interns who read proof including Mariyah Black, Hunter A. Blair, Lyndsey M. Clarke, Maddy Connelly, Anisah Dean, Emily E. DeNote, Nicole A. Lanzoni, Emma M. Marsico, Suzanne A. Mcconlogue, Dontae McFadden, Autumn L. Mcgaster, Shannon G. McGivney, Victoria Orlowski, and Madison R. Szucsik.

Special thanks to the people who interviewed for my project and the book, by order of their appearance:

Harry Everham, Darrell Watson, Jen Andzeski, Paul Evans Pederson, Miss L, Dave Philips, Charles, Millie Hopkins, James Pullaro, Bob Baker, Arney, Rob, Indian Tom, Mary Bozarth-Carty, Jo Martelli, Wayne Archer, Elaine Goodman, Terry Schmidt, Paul W. Schopp, Mark Szutarski, Frank, Victoria Kushnir, Colleen Gorman, Bill Wasiowich, Paul Hemler, Steven Carty, and Stephen Soviczki.

I appreciate you sharing your thoughts and feelings openly and honestly with me. I appreciate that you allowed me into your world and let me understand some of the Piney lives and culture. I hope this project will spread some truth about the life and culture of the people of the Pine Barrens. I love you all!

I also would like to thank each person I met along my way in the Pine Barrens; the ones who were nice to me and the ones who weren't. I learned from all of you. Thank you!

I am grateful to the people of the Pine Barrens who create music and tell stories. To my fellow journalists who wrote about the history of the place, and to the historians and academic people who shared their knowledge. You have been an inspiration.

To the various Facebook groups about the Pine Barrens: "The Pine Barrens," "Jersey Pine Barrens," and "Piney Lives – Piney Life," and the platforms you provide for an array of discussions.

The End

Not really. This is just the tip of the iceberg depicting the Pine Barrens' culture and its people. There are layers upon layers of history and stories yet to be told. And this is without talking about the special ecological system and the unique natural environment.

To be continued

Bibliography

Augustine, Sarah E., Kiyomi E. Locker, Dennis McDonald, Ted Gordon, *Whitesbog, Images of America* (Arcadia Publishing, 2022).

Capuzzo, Jill P., "The Pinelands That Time Forgot," *New York Times*, 2019.

Coen, Jon, "Lucille's Country Cooking: Where Locals Come for Down-Home Cooking," *New Jersey Monthly* (December 2021).

Dennert, James Walter, "Henry Herbert Goddard," *The Embryo Project Encyclopaedia*, 2021.

Ewing, Sarah W. R., *Atsion: A Town of Four Faces* (Batsto Citizens Committee, 1979).

Goddard, Henry H., "Mental Tests and the Immigrant," *Journal of Delinquency* no. 2 (1917): 243–77.

Goddard, Henry H., *Human Efficiency and Levels of Intelligence* (Princeton NJ: Princeton University Press, 1920).

Johnson, Carl, and David Munn, Atlantic City library research, "Jersey Devil – fact or fiction?"

Kite, Elizabeth, "The Pineys, the 1913 Survey," in David S. Cohen, "The Origin of the Pineys: A Local History Legend," *Folklife Annual* (1985), 40–59.

Larson, Erik, "Jersey Roots: Children of the Pines: New Jersey's Proposal to Sterilize 'Pineys'," *App* June 2014.

McPhee, John, "The Pine Barrens," *The New Yorker*, November 1967.

"Mob Favours Pinelands for Burials," *The New York Times*, February 5, 1973.

Mott, Joel, "History of the Barrens" Pineland Commission.

New Jersey, *Pinelands People: The Human Response to the Natural*, www.nj.gov/pinelands/infor/educational/curriculum/pinecur/pphrne78.htmEnvironment.

Rozinski, Danielle, "Sound of the Jersey Pine Book," ALBERT HALL collection archive in Washington DC.

Ruset, Ben, "NJ Pine Barrens," November 20, 2007, www.njpinebarrens.com/.

Sannnito, Joseph, "Joe Mulliner: The Infamous Jersey Outlaw of the Late 1700s," *The Omega* (2021).

Smith, J. David, *Minds Made Feeble: The Myth and Legacy of the Kallikaks* (Rockville, MD: Aspen Systems, , 1985).

Southside Permaculture Park, "Lenape 'Permaculture': The Three Sisters," (January 31, 2019), southsidepermaculturepark.org/lenape-permaculture-the-three-sisters/.

Stockton University, Bjork Library, "Buzby's General Store: The Evolution of a Cultural Center," in the online exhibition *Come See for Yourself* (2014), blogs.stockton.edu/specialselections/buzby-collection/.

Taylor, Charles, *Sources of the Self: The Making of the Modern Identity* (Harvard University Press, 1992).

Wier, Sally, "White Deer the Legend and the Science," (March 2, 2015), bouldercountyopenspace.org/i/wildlife/white-deer/.

www.ingramcontent.com/pod-product-compliance
Lightning Source LLC
Chambersburg PA
CBHW041139170426
43199CB00023B/2923